PlayTime® Piano

Christmas

Level 1
5-Finger Melodies

This book belongs to: _____

Arranged by

Nancy and Randall Faber

Production: Frank and Gail Hackinson
Production Coordinator: Marilyn Cole
Design: Terpstra Design, San Francisco
Engraving: Tempo Music Press, Inc.

FABER
PIANO ADVENTURES®

3042 Creek Drive
Ann Arbor, Michigan 48108

A NOTE TO TEACHERS

PlayTime® Piano Christmas is a collection of favorite Christmas songs arranged for the beginning pianist. For special student appeal, the book features both the well-known Christmas carols and the popular Christmas favorites.

The arrangements use primarily 5-finger hand positions for simplicity, yet extend enough beyond middle C position to reinforce note reading and interval recognition.

PlayTime® Piano Christmas is part of the *PlayTime® Piano* series arranged by Faber and Faber. "PlayTime" designates Level 1 of the *PreTime®* to *BigTime®* Supplementary Library, and it is available in a variety of styles including Children's Songs, Christmas, Classics, Favorites, Hymns, Jazz & Blues, Popular, More Popular, and Rock 'n Roll.

Following are the levels of the supplementary library which lead up to *BigTime®.*

PreTime® Piano	(Primer Level)
PlayTime® Piano	(Level 1)
ShowTime® Piano	(Level 2A)
ChordTime® Piano	(Level 2B)
FunTime® Piano	(Level 3A – 3B)
BigTime® Piano	(Level 4)

Each level offers books in a variety of styles, making it possible for the teacher to offer stimulating material for every student. For a complimentary detailed listing, e-mail faber@pianoadventures.com or write us at the mailing address below.

Visit **www.PianoAdventures.com**.

Teacher Duets

Optional teacher duets are a valuable feature of the *PlayTime® Piano* series. Although the arrangements stand complete on their own, the duets provide additional fullness of harmony and rhythmic vitality. And not incidentally, they offer the opportunity for parent and student to play together.

Helpful Hints:

1. The student should know his or her part thoroughly before the teacher duet is used. Accurate rhythm is especially important.

2. Harmony notes in the student part may be omitted if a steady rhythm is difficult to achieve.

3. Rehearsal numbers are provided to give the student and teacher starting places.

4. The teacher may wish to count softly a measure before beginning, as this will help the ensemble.

ISBN 978-1-61677-002-0

TABLE OF CONTENTS

4

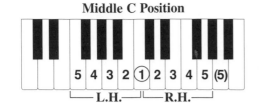

Middle C Position

Jingle Bells

Words and Music by
J. PIERPONT

With excitement

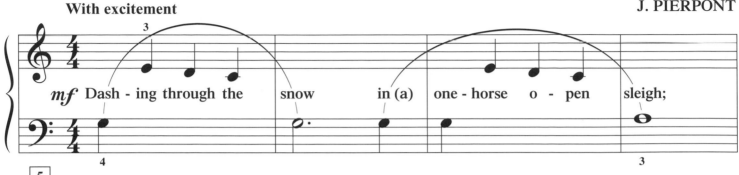

mf Dash - ing through the snow in (a) one - horse o - pen sleigh;

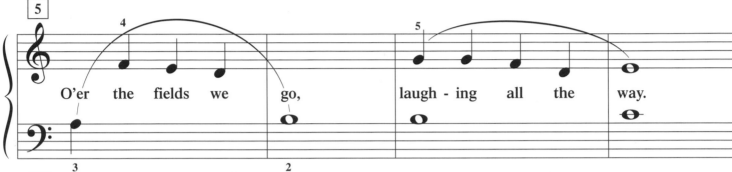

5

O'er the fields we go, laugh - ing all the way.

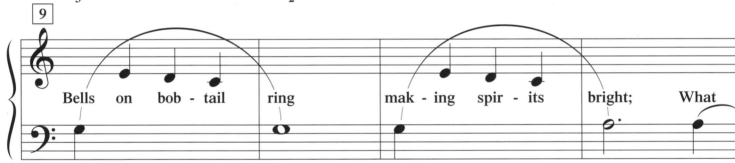

9

Bells on bob - tail ring mak - ing spir - its bright; What

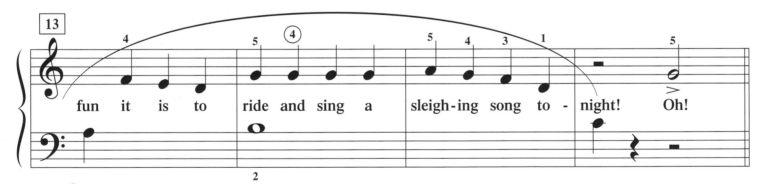

13

fun it is to ride and sing a sleigh-ing song to - night! Oh!

Teacher Duet: (Student plays 1 octave higher)

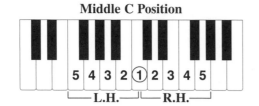

Middle C Position

O Come, All Ye Faithful
(Adeste Fideles)

Transcribed by F. OAKELEY
WADE'S "CANTUS DIVERSI"

Boldly

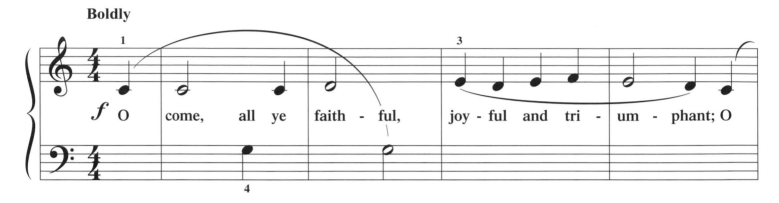

f O come, all ye faith - ful, joy - ful and tri - um - phant; O

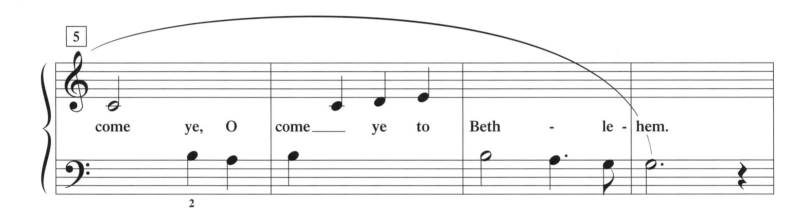

come ye, O come____ ye to Beth - le - hem.

Teacher Duet: (Student plays 1 octave higher)

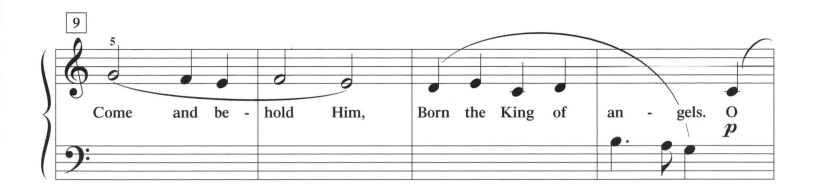

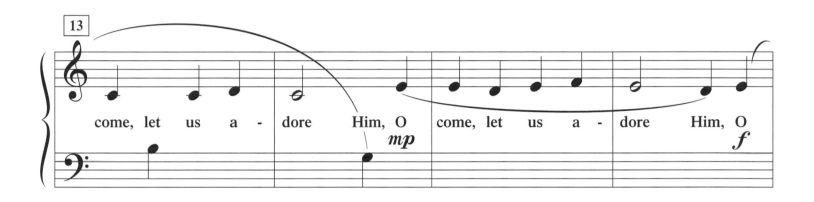

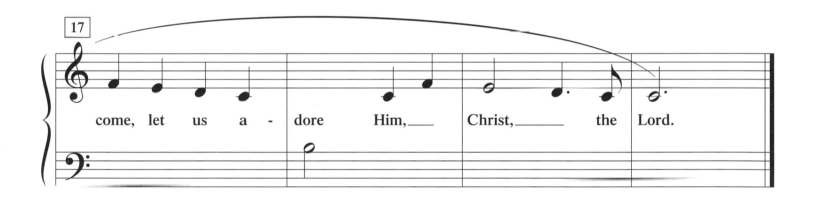

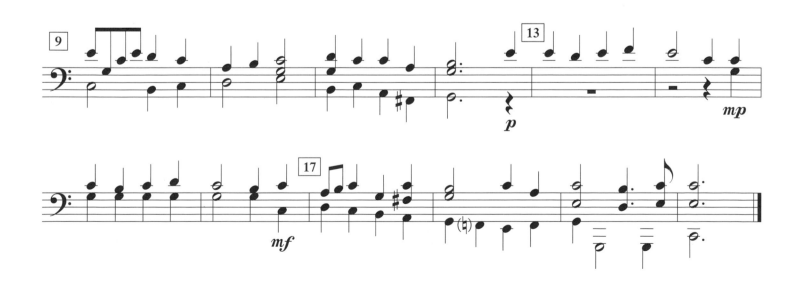

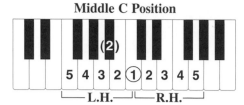

Middle C Position

When Santa Claus
Gets Your Letter

Music and Lyrics by
JOHNNY MARKS

Cheerfully

When San-ta Claus gets your let-ter, you know what he will say: "Have

you been good the way you should on ev-'ry sin-gle day?" When

San-ta Claus gets your let-ter, to ask for Christ-mas toys, He'll

take a look in his good book he keeps for girls and boys. He'll

Teacher Duet: (Student plays 1 octave higher)

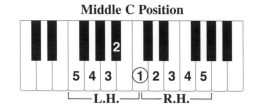

Silent Night

Words by JOSEPH MOHR
Music by FRANZ GRÜBER

Peacefully

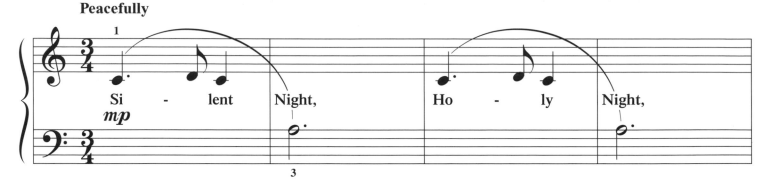

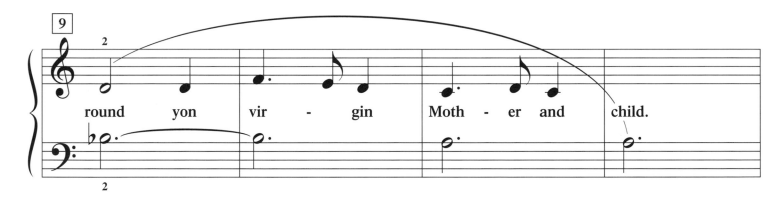

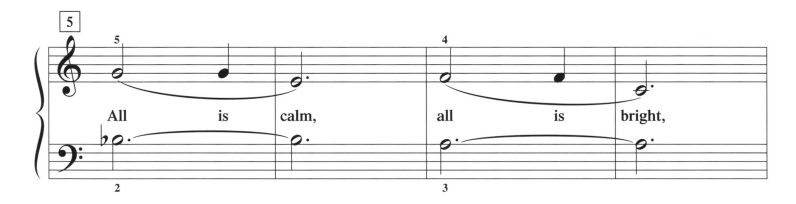

Teacher Duet: (Student plays 1 octave higher)

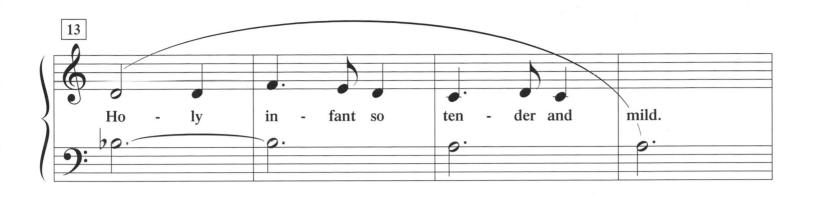

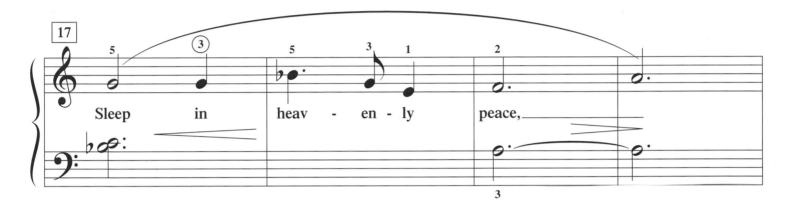

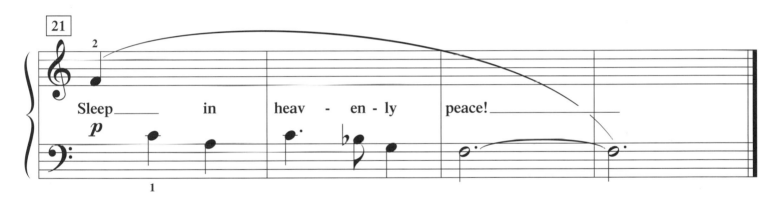

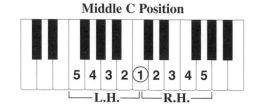

Middle C Position

Away in a Manger

JAMES R. MURRAY
Traditional

Gently

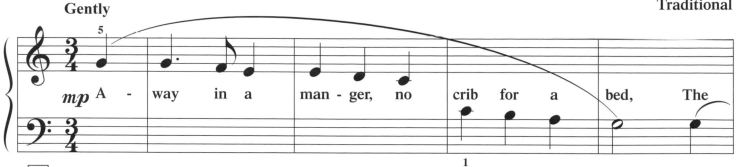

A - way in a man - ger, no crib for a bed, The

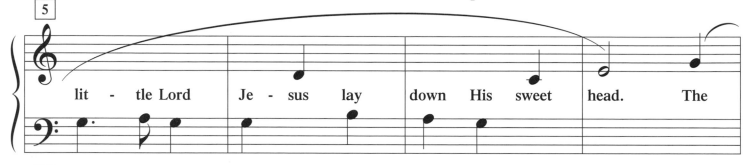

lit - tle Lord Je - sus lay down His sweet head. The

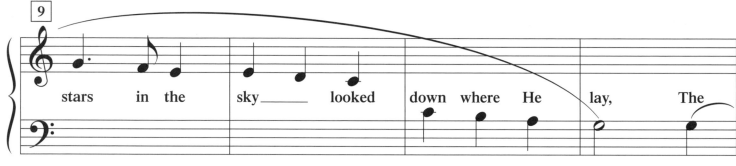

stars in the sky____ looked down where He lay, The

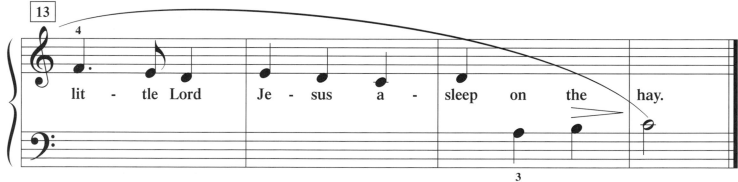

lit - tle Lord Je - sus a - sleep on the hay.

Teacher Duet: (Student plays 1 octave higher)

The First Noel

TRADITIONAL

Teacher Duet: (Student plays 1 octave higher)

FF1002

14

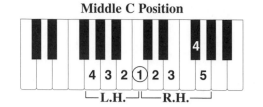

Middle C Position

Joy to the World

Words by ISAAC WATTS
Music by G.F. HANDEL

Joyfully

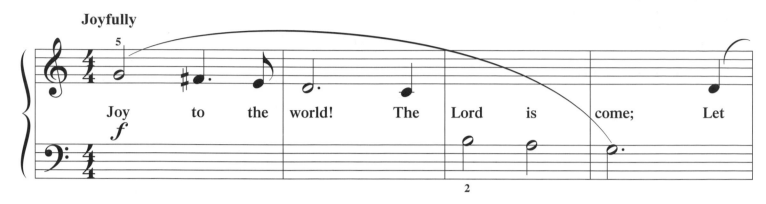

Joy to the world! The Lord is come; Let

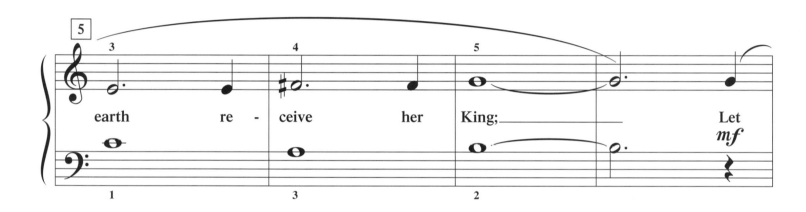

earth re - ceive her King; Let

Teacher Duet: (Student plays 1 octave higher)

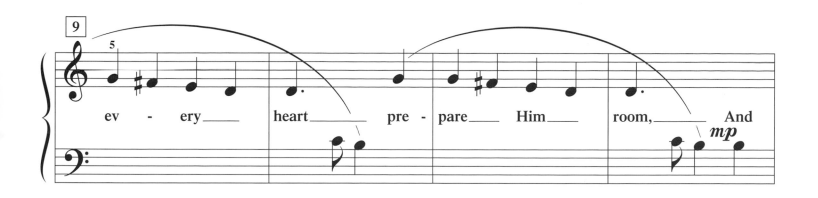

ev - ery___ heart___ pre - pare___ Him___ room,___ And

heav'n and na - ture___ sing, And___ heav'n and na - ture___ sing, And___

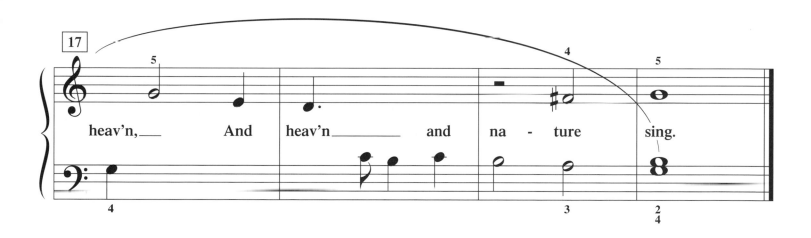

heav'n,___ And heav'n___ and na - ture sing.

16

Middle C Position

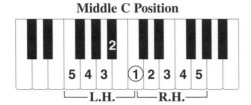

Rudolph the
Red-Nosed Reindeer

Music and Lyrics by
JOHNNY MARKS

Playfully

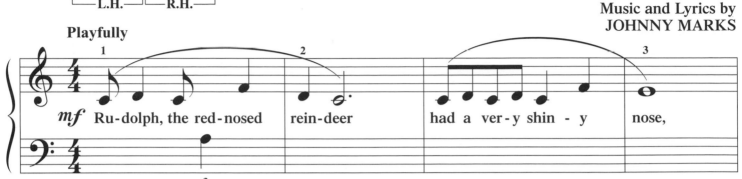

Ru-dolph, the red-nosed rein-deer had a ver-y shin-y nose,

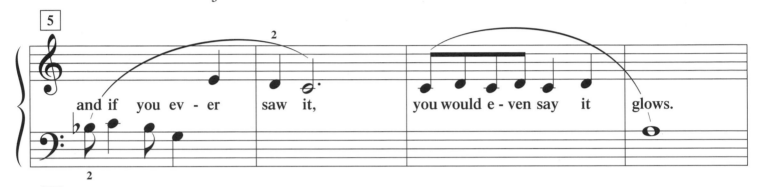

and if you ev-er saw it, you would e-ven say it glows.

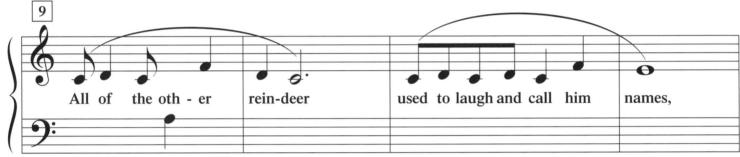

All of the oth-er rein-deer used to laugh and call him names,

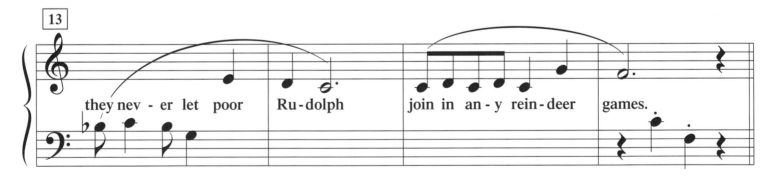

they nev-er let poor Ru-dolph join in an-y rein-deer games.

Teacher Duet: (Student plays 1 octave higher)

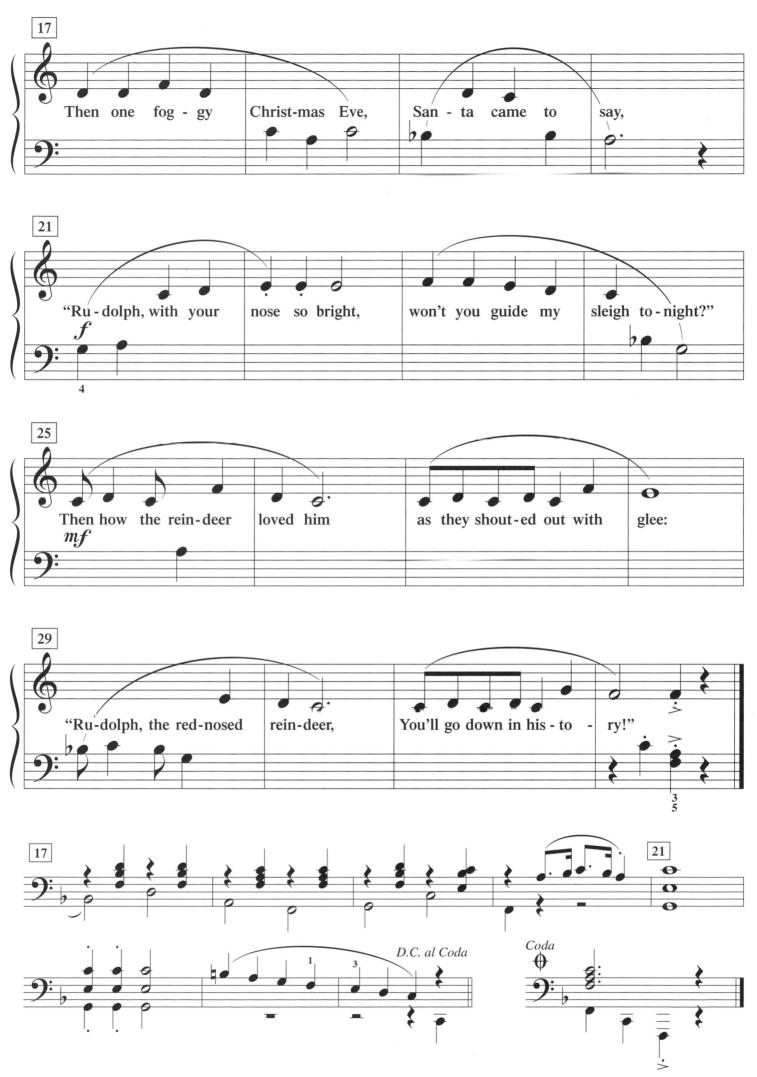

18

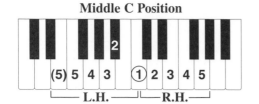

Middle C Position

A Holly Jolly Christmas

Music and Lyrics by
JOHNNY MARKS

With a happy feeling

Have a   Hol-ly   Jol-ly   Christ-mas,   It's the   best time of the   year.

move ⑤ to E

I   don't know if   there'll be snow, but   have a cup of   cheer.   Have a

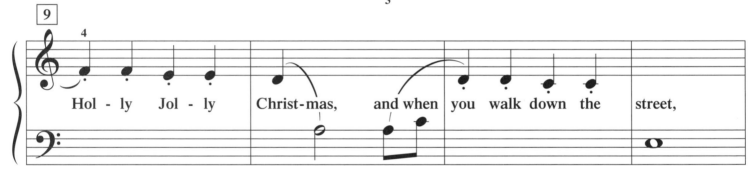

Hol-ly   Jol-ly   Christ-mas,   and when you walk down the   street,

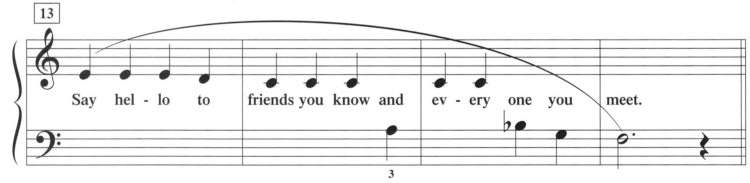

Say hel-lo to   friends you know and   ev-ery one you   meet.

Teacher Duet: (Student plays 1 octave higher)

FF1002

19

17 Oh, ho, the mis - tle - toe hung where you can see.

21 Some - bod - y waits for you, kiss her once for me. Have a

25 Hol - ly Jol - ly Christ-mas, and in case you did - n't hear,

29 Oh by gol - ly, have a Hol - ly Jol - ly Christ-mas this year.

FF1002

Middle C Position

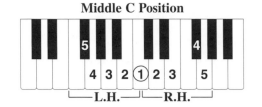

The Night Before Christmas Song

Music by JOHNNY MARKS
Lyric adapted by JOHNNY MARKS
From Clement Moore's Poem

Cheerfully

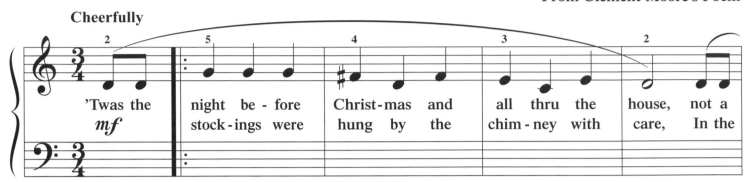

'Twas the / night be - fore / Christ - mas and / all thru the / house, not a
mf
stock - ings were / hung by the / chim - ney with / care, In the

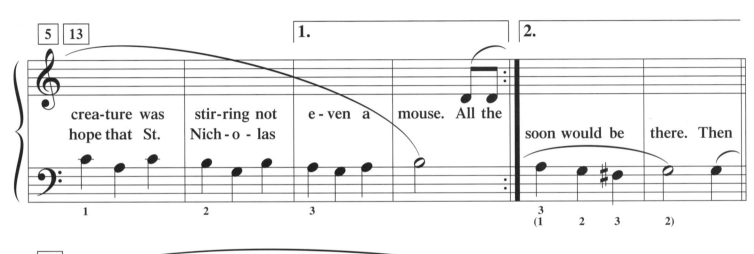

crea - ture was / stir - ring not / e - ven a / mouse. All the
hope that St. / Nich - o - las

soon would be / there. Then

what to my / won - der - ing / eyes should ap - / pear, A

Teacher Duet: (Student plays 1 octave higher)

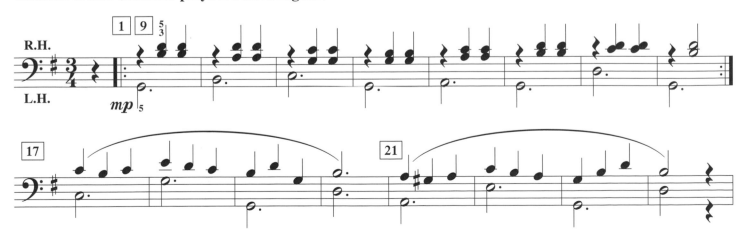

R.H.

L.H.
mp

FF1002

Rockin' Around the Christmas Tree

Music and Lyrics by
JOHNNY MARKS

With a great beat

Rock-in' a - round the Christ-mas tree at the Christ-mas par - ty hop.

Mis-tle-toe hung where you can see every cou - ple tries to stop.

Rock-in' a - round the Christ-mas tree let the Christ-mas spir - it ring.

Lat-er we'll have some pun - kin pie and (we'll) do some car - ol - ing.

Teacher Duet: (Student plays 1 octave higher)

To Coda

FF1002

We Wish You a Merry Christmas

TRADITIONAL ENGLISH CAROL

Teacher Duet: (Student plays 1 octave higher)